Northern Refuge

A Story of a
Canadian Boreal Forest

by Audrey Fraggalosch

Illustrated by Crista Forest

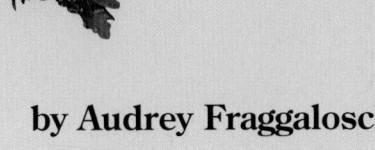

Soundprints
Where Children Discover...

To Helen, with gratitude — A.F.

To The Friends of Algonquin Park — C.F.

Book layout: Diane Hinze Kanzler
Editor: Judy Gitenstein

First Edition 1999
10 9 8 7 6 5 4 3 2 1
Printed in Hong Kong

Acknowledgments:
   Our thanks to Dr. James Peek, professor of wildlife resources at the University of Idaho
for his curatorial review.

Library of Congress Cataloging-in-Publication Data

Fraggalosch, Audrey
    Northern refuge: a story of a Canadian boreal forest / written by Audrey Fraggalosch;
illustrated by Crista Forest.
        p.   cm.
    Summary: A moose cow feeds, protects, and teaches her calf from the time of his birth
until he is a yearling and must begin to live on his own.
    ISBN 1-56899-678-0 (hardcover)   ISBN 1-56899-679-9 (pbk.)
    1. Moose — Juvenile fiction. [1. Moose — Fiction.] I. Forest, Crista, ill.   II. Title.
PZ10.3.F837   1999
[Fic] — ddc21   98-13023
                                                                                    CIP
                                                                                    AC

Northern Refuge

A Story of a Canadian Boreal Forest

by Audrey Fraggalosch

Illustrated by Crista Forest

The
Nature
Conservancy®

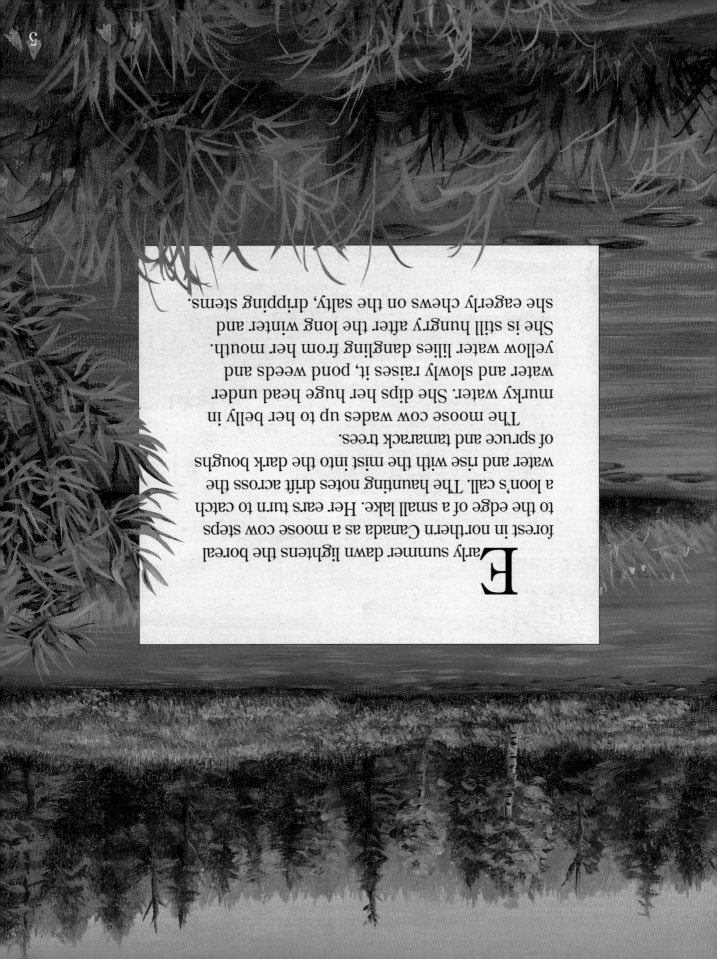

Early summer dawn lightens the boreal forest in northern Canada as a moose cow steps to the edge of a small lake. Her ears turn to catch a loon's call. The haunting notes drift across the water and rise with the mist into the dark boughs of spruce and tamarack trees.

The moose cow wades up to her belly in murky water. She dips her huge head under water and slowly raises it, pond weeds and yellow water lilies dangling from her mouth. She is still hungry after the long winter and she eagerly chews on the salty, dripping stems.

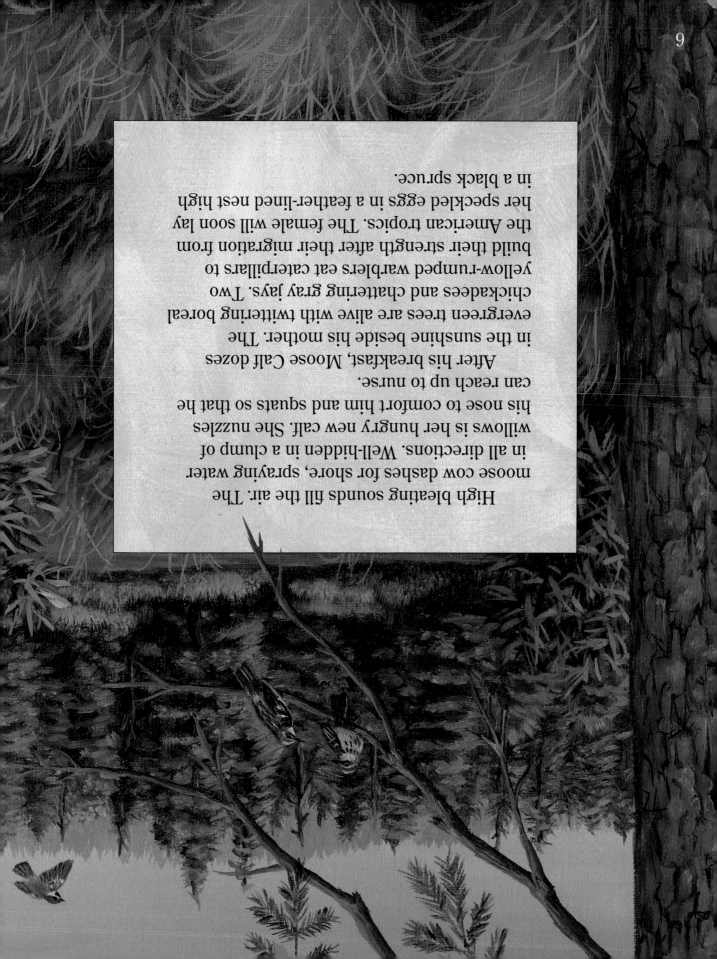

High bleating sounds fill the air. The moose cow dashes for shore, spraying water in all directions. Well-hidden in a clump of willows is her hungry new calf. She nuzzles his nose to comfort him and squats so that he can reach up to nurse.

After his breakfast, Moose Calf dozes in the sunshine beside his mother. The evergreen trees are alive with twittering boreal chickadees and chattering gray jays. Two yellow-rumped warblers eat caterpillars to build their strength after their migration from the American tropics. The female will soon lay her speckled eggs in a feather-lined nest high in a black spruce.

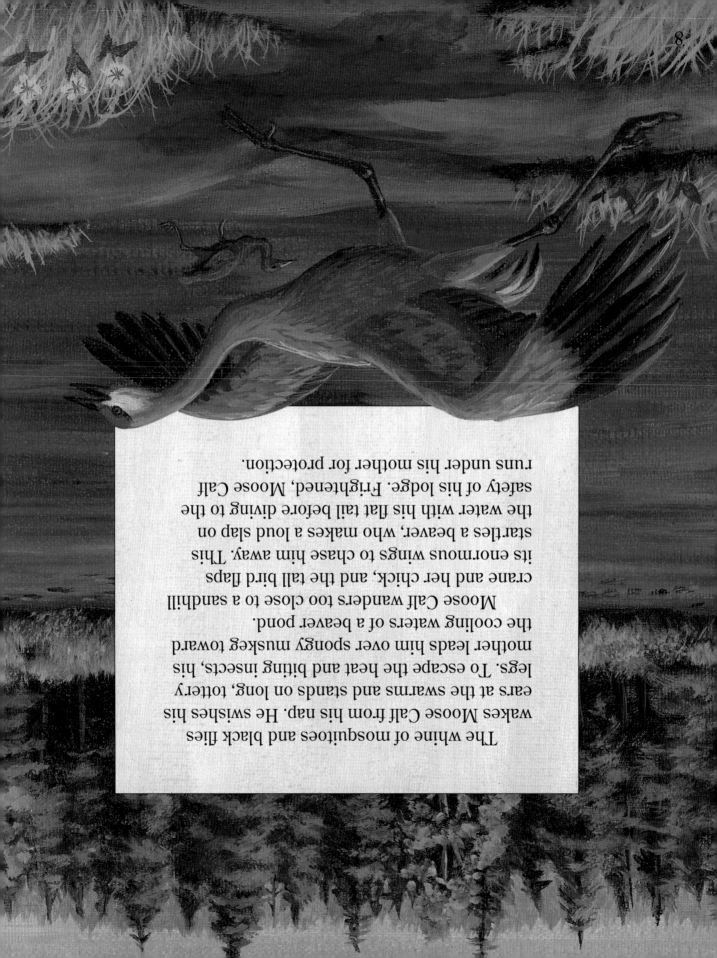

The whine of mosquitoes and black flies wakes Moose Calf from his nap. He swishes his ears at the swarms and stands on long, tottery legs. To escape the heat and biting insects, his mother leads him over spongy muskeg toward the cooling waters of a beaver pond.

Moose Calf wanders too close to a sandhill crane and her chick, and the tall bird flaps its enormous wings to chase him away. This startles a beaver, who makes a loud slap on the water with his flat tail before diving to the safety of his lodge. Frightened, Moose Calf runs under his mother for protection.

Moose Calf's mother licks him reassuringly. She grunts softly for him to follow her into the pond for his first swim. Moose Calf wades into the water up to his shoulders, then stops. Unsure, he begins to whimper. His mother calls again. She waits patiently until he gets up the courage to wade in deeper.

The water begins to close over his head and Moose Calf paddles hard. He is swimming! He paddles toward his mother, who is near a pair of Canada geese and their downy yellow goslings.

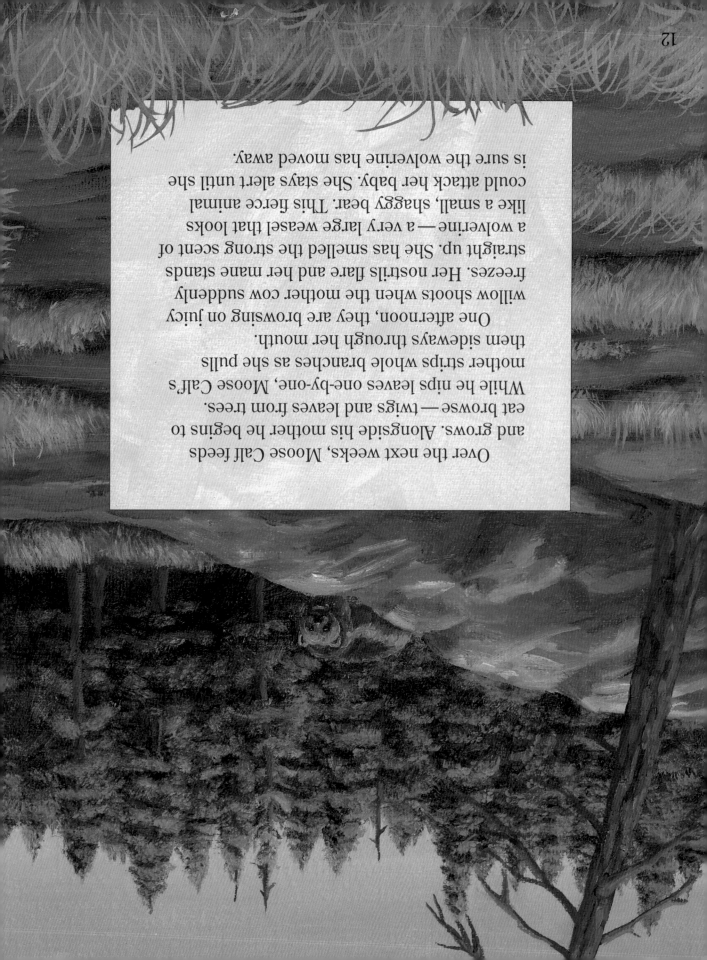

Over the next weeks, Moose Calf feeds and grows. Alongside his mother he begins to eat browse — twigs and leaves from trees. While he nips leaves one-by-one, Moose Calf's mother strips whole branches as she pulls them sideways through her mouth.

One afternoon, they are browsing on juicy willow shoots when the mother cow suddenly freezes. Her nostrils flare and her mane stands straight up. She has smelled the strong scent of a wolverine — a very large weasel that looks like a small, shaggy bear. This fierce animal could attack her baby. She stays alert until she is sure the wolverine has moved away.

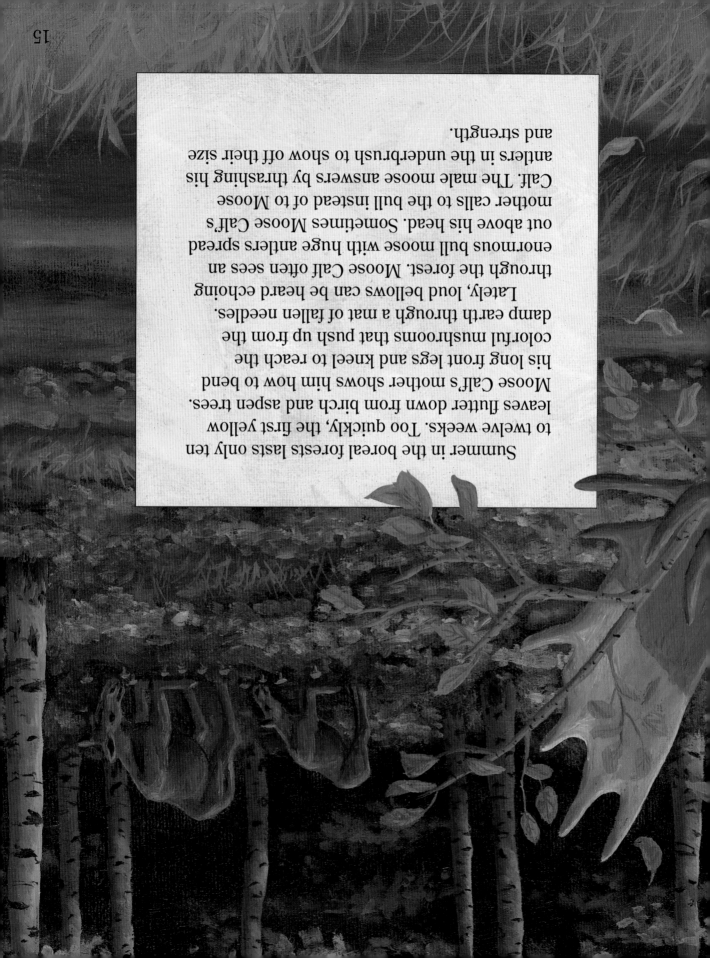

Summer in the boreal forests lasts only ten to twelve weeks. Too quickly, the first yellow leaves flutter down from birch and aspen trees. Moose Calf's mother shows him how to bend his long front legs and kneel to reach the colorful mushrooms that push up from the damp earth through a mat of fallen needles. Lately, loud bellows can be heard echoing through the forest. Moose Calf often sees an enormous bull moose with huge antlers spread out above his head. Sometimes Moose Calf's mother calls to the bull instead of to Moose Calf. The male moose answers by thrashing his antlers in the underbrush to show off their size and strength.

One crisp, fall afternoon, another bull breaks through the trees. He startles a red squirrel as it gathers spruce cones for winter food. This younger bull has also heard the calls of Moose Calf's mother. Ears back and eyes bulging, the two giant bulls tip their heads to show their antlers. The first bull lunges. With a crash, the bulls lock antlers and push hard! Again and again they clash. Finally, the younger bull is shoved back and he runs away.

The larger bull stays nearby until Moose Calf's mother is ready to mate. After that, he will disappear into the forest. Except for mating time, adult bulls live mostly by themselves.

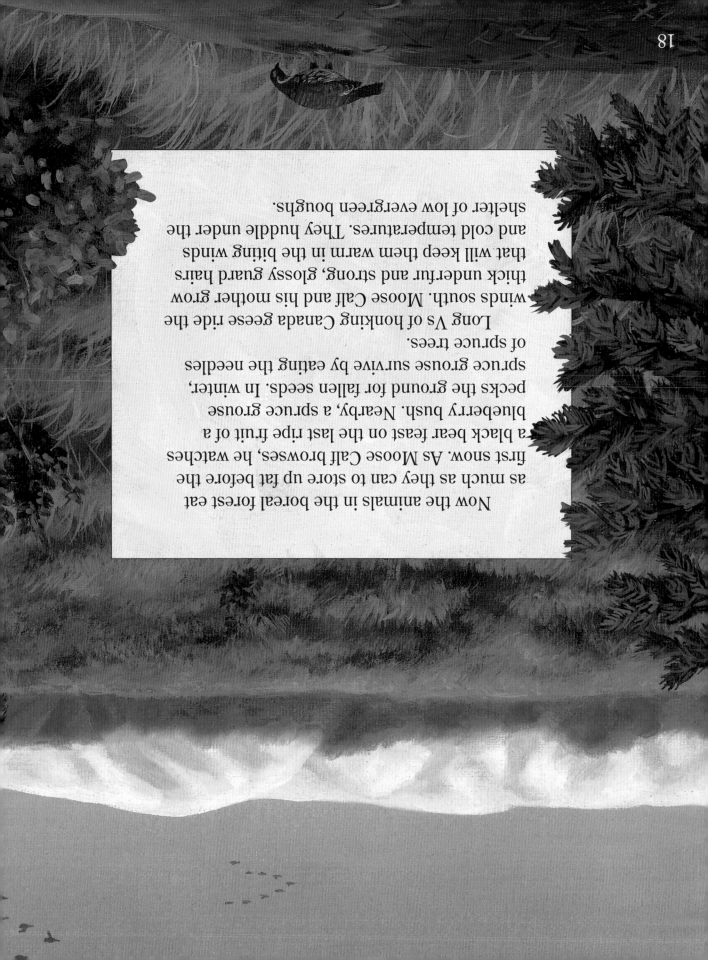

Now the animals in the boreal forest eat as much as they can to store up fat before the first snow. As Moose Calf browses, he watches a black bear feast on the last ripe fruit of a blueberry bush. Nearby, a spruce grouse pecks the ground for fallen seeds. In winter, spruce grouse survive by eating the needles of spruce trees.

Long Vs of honking Canada geese ride the winds south. Moose Calf and his mother grow thick underfur and strong, glossy guard hairs that will keep them warm in the biting winds and cold temperatures. They huddle under the shelter of low evergreen boughs.

Weeks have passed. Much powdery snow has
fallen. At night, northern lights flicker and flash
overhead in ribbons of soft green and purple.
A wolf howls. A shriek is heard as a lynx catches
a snowshoe hare. Now, wolves wail closer to
Moose Calf and his mother—too close!

Twelve yellow eyes appear in the dancing
shadows. Frosty breath puffs from the snouts
of six yelping gray wolves. Terrified, Moose Calf
runs. His mother follows, putting herself between
the hungry wolves and her calf. The long-legged
moose gain speed, kicking up clouds of fluffy
snow. With no frozen crust to run on, the wolves
begin to flounder in the drifts and Moose Calf and
his mother escape into the night.

Snow piles higher in the boreal forest. Moose Calf and his mother wade through drifts as they look for balsam fir twigs to eat, but it is hard now to find any browse. Moose Calf gets so hungry that he strips bark off trees with his teeth.

A northern hawk owl watches a porcupine gnaw on a large antler. Cast-off antlers make good winter food for porcupines, squirrels, and mice. The owl tenses. Its keen hearing has picked up sounds of movement under the drifts. The owl drops down and plunges its sharp talons into the snow to catch a tunneling deer mouse.

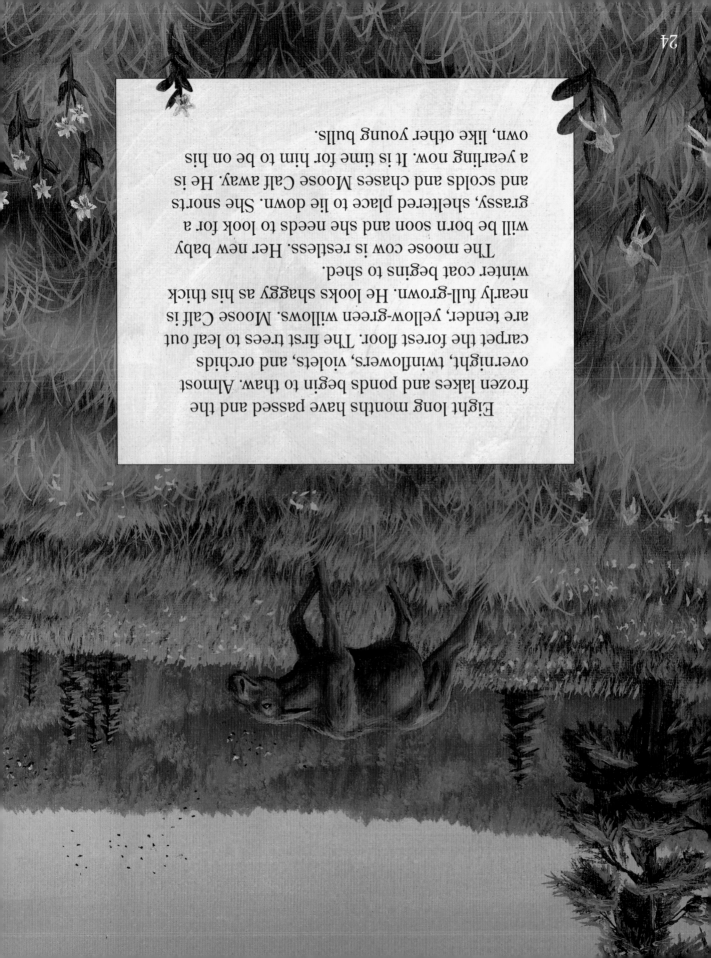

Eight long months have passed and the frozen lakes and ponds begin to thaw. Almost overnight, twinflowers, violets, and orchids carpet the forest floor. The first trees to leaf out are tender, yellow-green willows. Moose Calf is nearly full-grown. He looks shaggy as his thick winter coat begins to shed.

The moose cow is restless. Her new baby will be born soon and she needs to look for a grassy, sheltered place to lie down. She snorts and scolds and chases Moose Calf away. He is a yearling now. It is time for him to be on his own, like other young bulls.

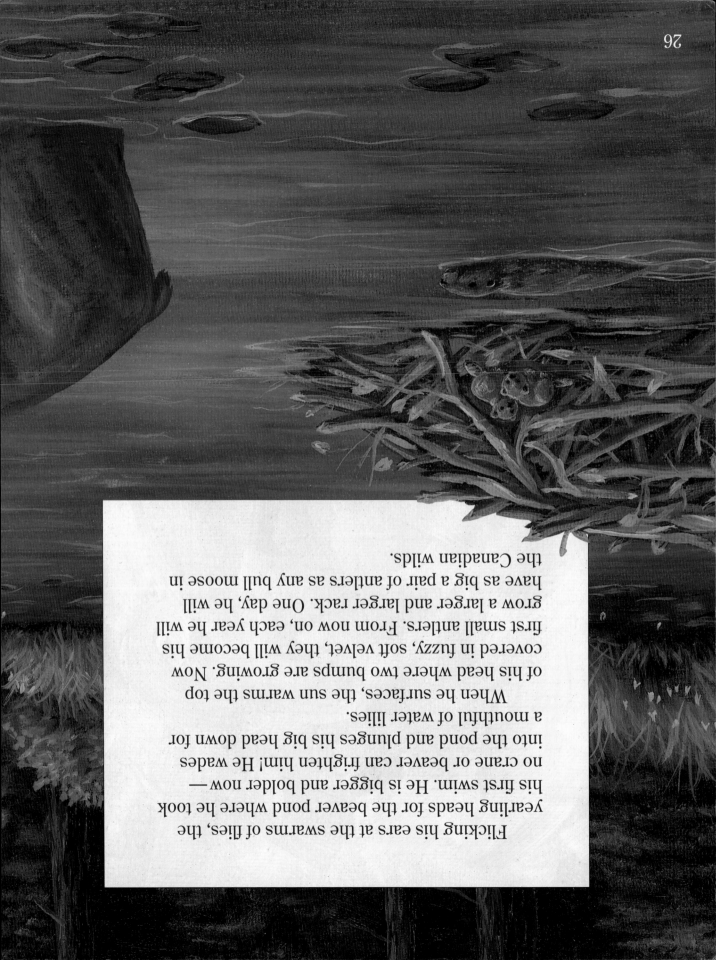

Flicking his ears at the swarms of flies, the yearling heads for the beaver pond where he took his first swim. He is bigger and bolder now — no crane or beaver can frighten him! He wades into the pond and plunges his big head down for a mouthful of water lilies.

When he surfaces, the sun warms the top of his head where two bumps are growing. Now covered in fuzzy, soft velvet, they will become his first small antlers. From now on, each year he will grow a larger and larger rack. One day, he will have as big a pair of antlers as any bull moose in the Canadian wilds.

Glossary

▲ *Aspen trees*

▲ *Gray wolf*

▲ *Bullhead-lily pads*

▲ *Black bear*

▲ *Lynx*

▲ *White spruce tree*

▲ *Black spruce*

▲ *Mosquitoes and black flies*

▲ *Wild blueberry bush*

▲ *Canada goose and goslings*

▲ *Porcupine*

▲ *Yellow-rumped warbler*

▲ *Spruce grouse*

About the Canadian Boreal Forest

The largest forest region in North America, the boreal forest is dotted with thousands of small ponds and lakes found in dents and hollows on the earth's surface left behind by glaciers fifteen thousand years ago. Over time, many of these hollows slowly filled in with waterlogged mosses and other decaying plant matter to form a type of swampland called muskeg. Neither land nor water, muskeg is a spongy mix of the two. In Canada, hundreds of thousands of acres of muskeg are found throughout the boreal forest. Along with other wetlands, muskeg provides vital habitat for many kinds of wildlife.

The boreal forest is moose country. Moose are the world's largest deer and the bull, or male moose, is the mightiest antlered animal. (Female moose do not grow antlers.) Bull moose stand about seven feet tall at the shoulder and measure about nine-and-one-half feet long. During the short northern summer, a full-grown bull moose eats sixty to seventy pounds of leaves and tender branches (known as "browse") per day to maintain a weight of around one thousand four hundred pounds.

Bulls shed their antlers each winter and sprout a new pair every spring. At first the antlers are covered by "velvet," a layer of skin with short, soft fuzz that protects and nourishes the growing antlers. This layer peels away in early autumn, falling off in ragged shreds. A yearling moose's first antlers may be six- to eight-inch prongs, small forks, or small hand-shaped "palms" with two or three points. A mature bull's antlers might span six-and-one-half feet.

Moose calves stay with their mothers for at least one year, or until the mother has another calf. The first time a moose cow has a baby it is usually a single calf; after that she will often have twins.

Moose and animals such as wolves, black bears, wolverines, and lynx, were once found more widely throughout other forest regions of the northern United States and Canada. People now think of them as typical only of the boreal forest. As human population and industry spread, the boreal forest is the last place in North America where wildlife can still find enough area to roam freely. To enable these animals and other species to survive, it is important that the ecology of the boreal forest is properly conserved and managed. In this way, the moose and other northern animals, birds, and other species will continue to survive in the Canadian wilds.

The Canadian Boreal Forest, North America

The boreal forest extends across Canada from the Atlantic
to the Pacific Ocean and up to Alaska. This huge northern region
has long, cold winters, a short growing season, and dark, coniferous—
or cone-producing—evergreen forests. There are few tree species,
mostly black and white spruce, balsam fir, jack pine, and tamarack.

▲ Beaver and lodge

▲ Deer mouse

▲ Sandhill crane
and nest

▲ Boreal chickadee

▲ Gray jay

▲ Twinflowers

▲ Bull moose

▲ Sandbar willow

▲ Wild mushrooms

▲ Canada violets

▲ Northern hawk owl
in a paper birch tree

▲ Yellow lady's-slipper

▲ Common loon

▲ Red squirrel

▲ Wolverine